PENGUIN BOOKS

EMETT'S MINISTRY OF TRANSPORT

Rowland Emett first made his name in *Punch*, and his drawings collected from its pages appeared regularly in book form in the forties and early fifties under such titles as *Saturday Slow* and *Buffers End*. His work during this period reached its apotheosis when Nellie the Engine puffed off the printed page and into the Battersea Pleasure Gardens as part of the Festival of Britain in 1951. Since then he has been creating a series of 'Things' for a number of large firms, films, shopping centres and museums. These range from the Forget-Me-Not Computer (an elephant with woodpecker punch-card operators, for Honeywell) to the Vintage Car of the Future (for Borg Warner). Since his machines can at best be seen as a peculiarly subversive form of alternative technology and at worst as an outright attack on the unacceptable face of Capitalism, one must respect the ability of his corporate-sponsors to laugh at themselves. He may say he lives at The Flanges, Gently-round-the-Bend, or The Bicycle Shed, Wisteria Halt, but in fact Rowland Emett lives in Sussex.

Emett's Ministry of Transport

Selected from

THE EARLY MORNING MILK TRAIN

and

ALARMS AND EXCURSIONS

PENGUIN BOOKS

Penguin Books Ltd, Harmondsworth, Middlesex, England
Penguin Books, 625 Madison Avenue, New York, New York 10022, U.S.A.
Penguin Books Australia Ltd, Ringwood, Victoria, Australia
Penguin Books Canada Ltd, 2801 John Street, Markham, Ontario, Canada L3R 1B4
Penguin Books (N.Z.) Ltd, 182–190 Wairau Road, Auckland 10, New Zealand

Selected from *The Early Morning Milk Train* (first published by John Murray
(Publishers) Ltd 1976) and *Alarms and Excursions* (first published by John Murray
(Publishers) Ltd 1977)
This selection first published 1981

The pictures in this book are reproduced from *Punch* by kind permission
of the Proprietors

Made and printed in Great Britain by
Butler & Tanner Ltd, Frome and London

"Some footling nonsense about a right of way, or something ..."

"… *shan't be sorry when I retire* …"

"I keep TELLING him we've done away with First Class!"

"Bother – it's a smoker!"

"*...and then they bring out this Pooling of Rolling Stock business.*"

"When are you going to see the Directors about a luggage-van?"

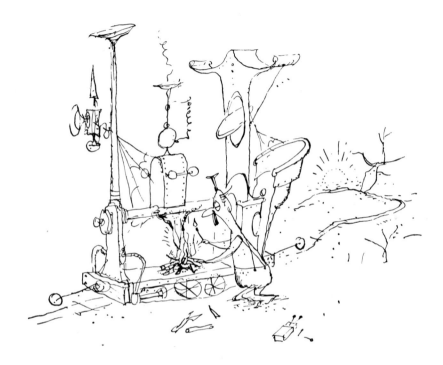

Steam raising, early morning

"Something to do with the nationalization of railways, I expect."

"Here's the 9.15. I see they've taken it off."

"I wish they'd have their Board Meetings when they GET to Town!"

"...he says very poor – rub out, do again and see him after six..."

"*I should have gone easy with the heat at first.*"

"...and a plaguy great dish o' tay will not come amiss at Brighthelmstone, I'll warrant me."

"Between you and me, sir, we don't quite know where THAT line goes to . . ."

"...and I asked him for two seats facing the engine, and HE said well, there's a war on, but he'd see what he could do...."

"*Serving dinner on the trains again, I see.*"

"*Y-e-s ... there* WAS *a gale warning on the eight o'clock, but* THAT *was for shipping.*"

"We feel we ought to do SOMETHING to take their minds off THAT."

"Salmon or pheasant?"

"Ah, yes – chap from London was TELLING *me the Underground was pushing farther afield."*

" There you are – that's what they SAID *they'd do: Railways, Road Services and Canals, all lumped together."*

"Psst! Squatters in number three"

"'Electrification', they say: and gone, gone is the wonder and romance of the Iron Road!"

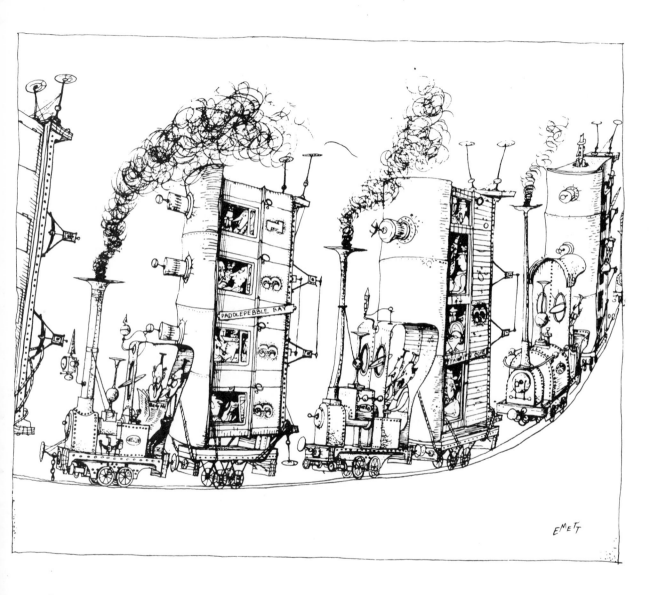

"*Just when we've found a way to crowd more holiday trains on the line – pfft! – ten per cent cut . . . !*"

"One in the eye for the Coal Board it MAY be, but have you thought about the Timber Controller?"

"*They say very sorry they'll have to have it back, but can offer in exchange desirable old-world property, detached, one up one down, balcony, positive sun-trap . . .*"

"Just a dress-rehearsal ... we're not going to get caught out THIS winter...!"

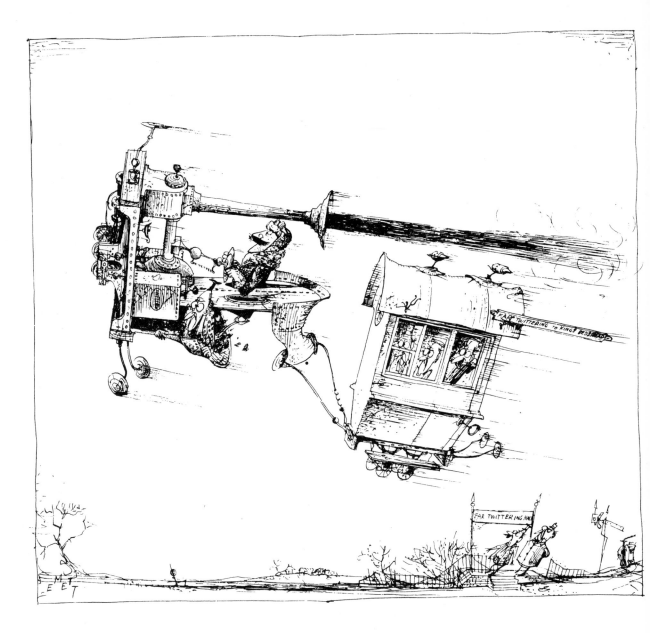

"*I'm not at all sure that the Labour Exchange has sent us the right sort of man for our stuff . . .*"

"*Granted the trains are slower than they were, and granted they use what rolling stock they can get,*
I STILL *think we're in the wrong train.*"

"Here's someone from the Government wants to see about making us part of the Network..."

"Oh well ...! season of mists and mellow fruitfulness ..."

" Yes, we're making a SPECIAL *bid for the American tourist business this summer . . ."*

"'Freak Magnetic Storm' the papers'll have it this evening..."

" *There you are, you see – a failing concern can always be revived with a spot of showmanship . . .* "

"Anyhow, we compelled him to observe the basic architectural rule of the district..."

"... with fares as they are, we're beginning to find we've got to TEMPT them ..."

"...but I do wish the Housing Committee and the Railway Extension people could have co-ordinated their plans!"

"A plague on these new double-deckers..."

"Winter service started, I see."

"Thank GOODNESS the kids have finally gone back to school...!"

"Well, I shan't be sorry when they put the 8.15 bus on again."

"...a little matter of the camel, the eye of the needle, and the basic petrol allowance, your Grace..."

"I said, the Englishman's traditional love of the sea is going to have serious consequences if you don't coax a few of them off the top."

"... now here we had a saying, 'all ship-shape'; but it seems to have lost its meaning lately."

"Of course, I know London's the hub of the Empire, and all that ..."

"Four bars of 'Good King Wenceslas' for each house is all we can manage this year."

"The Flying Squad, your Grace."

"Now I bet this makes YOU *homesick for Dead Man's Gulch ..."*

"Ah yes, I'd HEARD the Government might be going to take over the coal business."

"... Oh, and an eel for Mrs Mountford."

"Follow that car!"

"Now, my hearties! A rattling broadside of round-shot through his upper works!"

"A plague on this inadequate gas-pressure!"

"...and when they're withdrawn from service they need NO conversion."

"...but I DO wish we could have had one from the TOP of the heap."

"*Have* YOU *heard any of these silly stories about smuggling?*"

"Another of these wholesale stamp robberies!"

"... *If you care to step in a moment I'll just pop out and see if he's in the garden.*"

"Ah, HERE comes the Special Pantomime Bus!"

"There will be quite a few coming back now, I suppose..."

"*Now* THAT'S *the idea! If you're going in for this wind-on-the-heath stuff, do it properly . . .*"

"Full up inside ...... two only on top ...!"

"... and in view of the impending fuel cuts, I persuaded him to sub-let ..."

"We got a bit tired of Taplow, and thought we'd try Clacton for a change ..."

"I said, I've got a sneaking feeling they've let us have an Export Only model ..."

"Quick, boys! Steam-roller in the middle – tar-pressure up – chippings at the ready. I do believe there's a car coming ..."

"Nice to see the days of Chivalry and Enterprise aren't quite dead ..."

"Misses the 'bus practically EVERY morning, he does ..."

"It's not a subsidized line, but somehow they seem to make quite a decent profit."

"Can you really believe it? Here we are, actually drifting down the Grand Canal in a gondola, like the Doges of old!"

"THOUGHT *the old brigade wouldn't let those new nippy taxis get away with it . . .*"

"And they do say that somewhere on the farm is the site of a Roman amphitheatre."

"One thing about these power cuts, we can accommodate the whole of the queue."

"Ah, I THOUGHT *they'd have to cut down on those terribly expensive flying-boats and things . . ."*

"Load-shedding again, I see ..."

"There's something wrong with that machine!"

"Which way for the Edinburgh Festival?"

"*Yes, a plain potato lifter's all very well, but science can't stand still – we just had to complete the cycle.*"

"FRIGHTFUL *faux pas* ... *pretend you haven't seen it* ... 'Last Tram' Ceremony was last week, and then someone goes and discovers another one ..."

"I've heard of those things being used for crop-spraying, but ...!"

"*I told you that sign said 'Unsuitable for Motors' ...*"

"*I had an absolutely free hand with it, except for a few fiddling suggestions from the tram and telephone people.*"

"They've gone around like that ever since this talk of doing away with the trams ..."

"Still a few gentlemen farmers left, it appears."

"*No,* NOT *power cuts* ... *The trams cause some kind of interference.*"

"I TOLD you to keep a sharp look-out for souvenir hunters ...!"

"... and a rather neat arrangement with the County Council takes care of the expenses of my walking tour."

"There! I knew nobody would be silly enough to burn old tramcars."

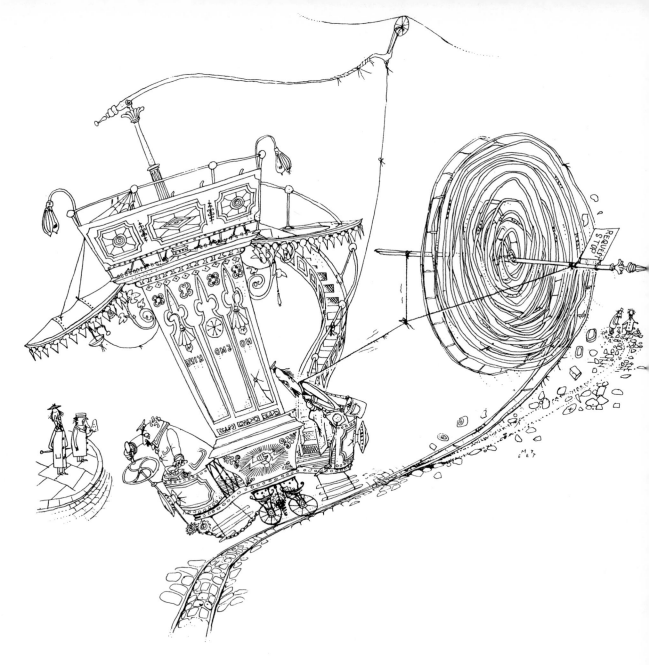

"*Well, I should say most definitely that really is the very last tram.*"